JUDITH KAZANTZIS

Let's Pretend

Published by VIRAGO PRESS Limited 1984
41 William IV Street, London WC2N 4DB

Copyright © Judith Kazantzis 1984

All rights reserved

British Library in Cataloguing Data
Kazantzis, Judith
  Let's pretend.
  I. Title
  821'.914   PR6061.A98
  ISBN 0-86068-630-2

Printed in Great Britain by
The Anchor Press, Tiptree, Essex
Photoset by Rowland Phototypesetting Limited
Bury St Edmunds, Suffolk

Some of the poems in this collection have appeared in *The Honest Ulsterman, Ambit, Siting Fires, New Departures, Kronos, Ninth Decade, Gallery.*

For I. W. . . . And for those who have
been true friends. And for my
parents, my true friends, with gratitude.

Contents

Grace	5
The wild girl	6
Picking up apples	9
The nurse's sorrow	10
Jack and the women	11
A Sussex lady	13
In the garden	14
Silver hands	15
The children mourn	16
Mrs Scott-Knight	17
At Mrs Leigh's	18
The humble beer	19
Research notes	20
The doorman	22
A thatcher	23
The ending we are projected	24
Anna Akhmatova	25
Heracles: a sketch	26
Troilus and Achilles	27
On the coast	28
The separation	31
The prince of the shining white character armour	32
Stars go up and down	33
Leaves	34
The cabin	34
The hypnotist's dream	35
The hawthorn	36
Look up, look out	37
Io the wanderer	38
Dark	41
Too far away	41
The river, the child	42
The loving red hen & the strong young fox	44

Up to a sea blue door	46
Leaves podgy stars	47
Gilbert's Motel	48
The pearly jawfish	49
Moon over Key West	50
Flipper at Key West	52
Key West dawn	53
Past an American classroom	54
Watching American TV	55
Said the judge	56
Vieux Carré	57
Let's pretend	58
What idiots lovers are	59
I said goodbye to you	60
The woman alone	62
As we might have done	64

Grace

Confessing my
pigtail of sins
to the priest's mild tone
and the wind behind the door,
that milky shining stuff
enwrapped my heart
like silver muslin
round a girl.

For five minutes, a half day,
like a meringue,
a bazaar prize,
a lambent angel cake,
I rose
in clean and steady warmth.

But the brick red oven leered
where you could not die
but fell, and whispered
together, as plump as chips
in rows on sizzle.

The flush
begins to swell
the white frail feeble gauze.
My shining wrapping
burns back, falls in
to flesh.

I have lost the stuff
called pure,
the temperate glow,

I am unconfessed.

The wild girl

1981: a ten-year-old Portuguese girl, Isabel Quaresma, was rescued from the family chicken run in which she had been kept since babyhood

1

Poor Isabel.   Your eyes
fill your face,
a face as small and jawless as a cat's.
Heavy of look.
One eye gone, milky, from a claw scratch.
Your arms that flap,
your drumming feet
express in hen fashion
surges of upset, or craving hunger.
You scratch for grain.

2

Long ago, lived the wild boy,
unearthed, snarling, from the forest
in the time of the Emperor
when mitre-hatted Grenadiers
pulled cannon
up white roads.
He too was hauled (with effort: it's said
he prefers all fours and his
meat raw)
into a half child's Christian life.
A sense of guilt was painfully
implanted.
But running out, he
whimpered at the moon.
He harks back, it's said, desolate
for his wolves . . .

A wall of mist on a deep pool early,
the beechcobs under his palms,
gliding to drink
and snuffling the wealth
of the black soil.

Imagine the free nursling.
Sharptoothed.
He dives into fern,
roams, behind eyes
barred among us.
It was long ago, and Europe
dense with forest.
Of parentage, after exhaustive inquiry
nothing known.

3

And Isabel.
Not long ago, your nursery floor
was shit, and exhausted earth.
Not long ago your sky was netting.
Perhaps the feathery breasts
gave you a soft view, a drowsy
sleep in the coop.
But also the parted beaks
would clatter,
the contracted claws
fan,
the beaks jib
at your unwrapped softness.

You call now, in high monotone
as they did.
Their eyes swivelled like red
counters, all
hemmed in prey.

4

Discs,
your eyes reflect outwards –
just the running quarrel
once a day
for the glittering grain
from the netted sky –
Though for some years, this
little and local wildlife
has been well known
roundabout:
this agreement with hens
to bring you up.

And what still throws, happily
the boy to the sharp blank
of wolves?
Is he our child of nature,
our tribute?
Are you his parody, merely
a child unnaturally hurt?

Picking up apples

Why pick rotten apples?
says my daughter
bending over,
her long hair drooping to the garden
– is it her economy,
her panic at what's wrong
(something below the nursery level
           of the world's hungry
which in her arrogance of sixteen
she sniffs at.
Not for her the unjust
rotten mountain.
Her brain's too clear, too unruffled.)

Why pick rotten apples?
She keeps her foothold on
a sea of weedy currents,
clearing the floor for her father's
           mysterious aches
grown from poverty, after all
on his own back door step
years and years ago; and still
active and virulent
           like a worm of fright
looking only to itself;
and she going to pick up apples
to save the lawn.

The nurse's sorrow

He is the old year,
you look at his sharp chin,
his shrivelled paunch like
a crabapple tightly
stranded in cold
wet brown grass.
He's as docile as a
fieldmouse, no idea
of enmity, just to be
friendly.   Beware him.
He'll tie you in grass
like swaddling
              because

he'd love a child,
he'll rock anybody walking.
All the livelong day.   But
the flowers on the
open hill are
blowing harder than he tells –
The sea is minstrel blue,
it falls down hundreds of feet
it rises up, it
lifts its arm, it
with a whirr fans the blank
chalk face, the cliff
hefts up its white bodiless face
on pinions.

All valley here, he says;
he clogs with violets
under the hedge.
All starlit night he
whispers the dawn chorus

to pacify his babe
(who is ineffably angry)
and to bring the promise
of a lovely day.
                       Isn't it

the cold heart
who'll tread down such kind
sorrow of the nurse?
Will you hush
in his cradle?
Here is
the bony frame: its
shadow, to
and fro on the grass.
                   O angry babe.

Jack and the women

He is frightened, hurrying home
frightened
hurrying in his straitened waistcoat:
he's nervous of gangs, and the big man
in overalls who pulls his arm
and asks for 10p till tomorrow:
Jack hands it over.

Under his vest the straitened
heart
his mother's face hangs
like a huge pill
(he had to take her)
so he likes his excitement dosed,
docile: we threw him behind

over our arrayed and newly positive shoulders,
he was wetting his pants,
a foundling in a bag in a hedge:
what can we get from a baby?

The man in the overalls
with the crewcut, dossing on the green grass
turns the park off, just like that –
the cedars go dreary,
the mallard mothers
lose their infants to dogs and foxes –
it happens all the time:
how often have I implored my friend Jack
to defend us.

Meantime, skulking in stiffened collar,
even flashing mildly behind
too thick rhododendrons: his prisms
(penis stays lulled and unprismatic)

His mother hangs her head, like a
gas balloon sinking on its string,
leaning over the azaleas, inquiring
for her high-strung boy:
we leave at once you hear
the language I declare I never – she
flounces upwards, in all
her born days . . .

Friend, I sneak to your hand
in the damp bushes.
You and I are pulled down,
we inch ourselves
and make our language, and stealthy . . .
in dark and retired areas,
we learn
such truanting!
Such mingling of tongues.

A Sussex lady

Channel clouds darken the flint farm.
They pass like long vehicles
over the dove cotes, over
the family of high-necked swans.

Remember the mermaid tail roofs
and the black-eyed chapel
of Lewes, like a duck
on a bank between the cars.
Remember the slur of the Ouse
towards and away from a deep
                      and obedient pond,
netted by road, wire, pole.
You can see the pure sports cars
seed in the valley
like lilies; from Beddingham Beacon.

I keep my voice up.
I speak from a vigorous throat.
My heart
misses a beat sometimes, but not
in the garden.
Nasturtiums grow like the faces
of my daughters,
                      quiet rioters.
They are green and weak
and go everywhere.

Mr Tanner is cutting down
his silvery weeping willow tree.
I drink from a Jubilee mug,
on yellowy green tweed
knees, my preferred tea.

And I watch the last sun go down
behind the elms.
The rooks are displaced yearly
onto lower,
less imperial,
less heartfelt trees.

I mean, the backwater
city of my head,
the locked up towers –
I have withdrawn my bowmen
and abandoned the flowery
                        maypole wards
for the squalor hits below the waist.

I walk the blue farmlands of the downs.
A kindly labrador nurses my heel.
There is the evening news
                        coming from the sea
in the swelling mist.
I run my finger along my arm, for dust.

In the garden

You paint me as a lily
head drooping,
needing to be staked.

I paint you as a wire
a convolvulus,
my head drooping.

Silver hands

Shielding my ego,
it's a tiny ego but monstrous,
from her critical eyes
though she looks away

to a horizon of pale blue
hills and ideal waves
glimmer of waves
at evening

She looks avaunt but
I know what she thinks
(I think) back through
tread of her ideal

to where my activities –
like the soil that is
full of ants, running and
apparently running, this way

and that – to where my
queenship burrows in
and disturbs the repose of
the matron, the madonna, the mother

the mother of the family –
What can I tell the great
world, I have no
silver hands, no fame.

The children mourn

The children mourn on the train.
Pigeons with ruby eyes
rock and purr with cries in their
stamped crates.

How can I get on with my thoughts –
She pleads, and pleats and unpleats the
                              travelling rug
laid over her knee.
Their shrieks where they are bowling
their slim planed hoops, and whipping
their trim tin tops,
these games resound down the corridor.

It lurches over a maze of points
through a labyrinthine weald
of village halts,
large named stops and starts.

Its wheels shriek.   At barriers cars,
knots of people with raised mouths:
where?   where?   Shouting after the
tail that bowls off sparks
into ravines of hushed trees.

The children mourn too loudly;
                    far too loud.
How can I open the lunch-basket
and dig in, as I need: a
roast fowl with sunken red eyes.
              – In such a kerfuffle
how can I make a meditation
such as I know I need?

Where shall I find in this rattle and sway,
my own soul
whose graceful and comforting arms
I do seriously need
in the face of the coming arrival?

He peers in through the darkened
racing carriage window
              as if he was floating
   level
                on wings.

Mrs Scott-Knight

Mrs Scott-Knight refuses all sustenance.

The vigour of her response
depends on the tennis.

A white band cramps her curls.

Her short brown arms
embrace the gracious, emerald trees
the planes, the ashes

– she encompasses all with
the catgut crisscross wave of
her white wand racket

and bends to measure the net
racket on racket

I love the snub nose of her short blonde face

and would respect those short hands' stroke
nor challenge Mrs S-K
in any part of the court.

At Mrs Leigh's

Under the tinned rhubarb sky
it's dark in Shepherd's Bush.
Tubes on the track purr through
and wind through the closed market
burrs down to my gas fire.

Upstairs they're playing guitar wisps
and gentle gestures.   Their shoes
squeak and pinch and tumble
overhead.   They visit the loo
as the train purrs; and the pipes sing

against the great soft roar beyond
the walled garden.   In that
dark orange clouded garden
in a homemade rubberised pond
five fish lie, of Mrs Leigh.

The humble beer

The humble beer at my right hand,
the fire a bar before my toe,
the television square ahead,
the sofa yielding to my rear,
the kettle pouting on the stove.

The sheriff switching smoking guns,
the tender chop upon the plate,
the fork to left, the knife to right.
The sheriff scolds the fiery whore,
the kettle pouting on the stove.

The bashful sheriff eyes the whore,
the knife and fork upon the chop,
the humble beer leaves little dregs,
the whore and sheriff ponder life,
the kettle whispers on the stove.

The sofa emanates a doze,
the fire recirculates my toes,
the whore and sheriff lose their clothes,
the tender chop inside me goes,
the kettle slumbers on the stove.

Research notes

Three men were observed
to play with a white faced monkey
in a playpen,
in their white coats.
One.   They lowered her.
Two.   They took notes.

There were her mouthings, her
scrabbling fingers, her twining arms.

The questions she raised
were debated, carefully
overhead.   You could see
eyes turned to each other, concentrated.

She turned and turned her head.
Her eyes dazzled up.

Noticeably
         she dangled short.
Her eyes levelled off at
the flat dark coat pocket
buttons, on the white coats.
The men broke her hold, which
continually seemed to
appear to threaten their pens
         or eyes.

We watched this silent film.
I saw the twin white moons
furred round each dark eye
imploring.   The monkey's lip
bared back with fear,

continuously she thrust up her
slender body and screamed at
the three men.   At length
they shocked the screeching
animal to death, so to
move to the next, so to
move to the truth: bright
                    truth
                 like a star
   sharp
as a fang.

The doorman

The doorman dreams of the door.
His hat is blue, braided
with hotel gold.
Today he opened the door
sometimes one way,
sometimes the other
with a smile apparent under
his moustache.
The double doors split before the guests
who sailed out or lapped home.
He moved before or behind
his grave moustache turning upwards
like a black November leaf.
He enlarged the door space fully
to give passage to the rapid guests.
In bed, to sleep, he counts
up the reversing swish.
One pull inwards, one pull outwards,
two inwards, two outwards
till he ebbs on a hoovered carpet
printed with whirlpools,
then flows to, on steel pivots
and sleeps and snores.

In the dream, his
shoulders are solid ice,
his hat wheels around lightly,
his teeth are huge glass panels
inside
that swing to, and grind
and swing back.

A thatcher

A thatcher is someone who makes a roof
or used to, when things were quieter,
was someone who sheltered people
from the rain, when things were quieter.
A thatcher took folks from the wind
and layered the skin of a human weather.
Now a thatcher exposes the dwellers,
rips off the roof in the skinning wind,
hurls down the roof on the dwellers,
who for cover snatch at the straws
the roof-maker rains
on their rainwashed heads ruthlessly
and in their teeth and in their eyes
like a war
that the thatcher unnaturally makes
on the dwellers.   And the luckier
snatching more straw cover of the undoing
thatch, despise the unluckier, the colder ones,
so that some see but many don't
or do see but not why, and think it
the way of a brave wise thatcher
that their fellows are icy and cold
in an inhuman country.

The ending we are projected

It denudes all partings,
all lovers whose fingers
ladder together, walking towards
the desert field,
all children who shout for the parent
who recedes through the wood
of scraped trees,
all parents who watch
their children leaf upwards
into outer air.

It demeans all who are old
and break breath like stones
to keep breath till breath breaks.
Draw curtain or not,
it means the blackening of the room.

We are used to going away,
trained to its regular sound
as regular as the heart
in its single casing.
We are handed out at birth
onto two full breasts, one pleasure
one grief, and grow between both.
But this projected parting
rejects all offers
fouls flow
poisons our mouths.
Childish or old
our goodbyes are made mad.

Our goings are tinged
and sucked into its rearing aura

where a one-eye gropes out –
It boils up dust, from which nothing.
It spits out a process of nothing
and us the projected grist.   We must
not let our griefs, our parted natures
be so annulled, so further emended;
we are ironclad and clouded over
to denuded and sour
dust and nothing.

Anna Akhmatova

Who with a reserved voice
spoke for dead
millions.   Who appointed herself.
Who prepared

with Fear and the Muse
standing watch by turn.
To speak the acknowledgement.

And incredible to me
the poet given and by herself
such valid graces, such statue

bronze-lidded by the Neva
where prison doves coo.
The killed voices, flying up, out
always.

Heracles: a sketch

Why him?
You may well ask –
the big man of the Olympic village,
sweatband star
siring on every passing sheep,
ever-ready with a ham hand of clubs
oak, knobkerry, thorn,
batman of the olive groves,
Yahoo of the Med,
the sort of a chap who,
burnt black from spatulate
big toe to bull
neck and brass forehead,
with chest of silvery hair,
sails to win;
gets from Piraeus to Smyrna
in two days there and back,
commandeers the local taverna
with a paunch laugh and
a wad of Athenian notes.
They all like him
knowing where Heracles
exactly, big toe to brass brow,
smile, wallet and club,
begins and ends.

Troilus and Achilles

Graves: The Greek Myths

'I will kill you,' he said,
'unless you yield to my caresses.'
'Troilus fled' as well he might
– before the Apollo haired
panting officer
his thighs shooting for goal,
his furry calves done up
in bulges,
his knees as huge as wheel hubs
revolving after Troilus
scampering ahead like elastic.

Troilus: pale olive waist unburned by
foreshore days of sweating,
a neat bearded boy
with black round eyes
who fought as taught, loved by
old sergeants who worried at his
lack of bone, but chuckled at
the grit of the small lad.

Now eaten with belches by Achilles
down to the last slender
memorabilia: a piece of heart
or a black round scared eye
to scare Briseis with
in the arms of Diomedes the Greek.
So golden Achilles passes on
seeking and flaying pale olive skins.

On the coast

1

On the coast
we do not float far from
our own concerns,
cutting the melons six ways
for breakfast at nine and twelve.

The children in the swimming pool
float there, legs
interwoven like whiskery
prawns, in unnatural blue.
Yesterday all day too.

And Chloe's hair
begins to change its do:
straight honey lines.
She tips her nose out,
flickers her frogskin eyes.

The boys below
chat unnatural science
over fetta and marmalade.
In the bay
a shark is felt to heel and go.

2

Occasionally, I think
he must dream of me
in a city far away
curving his full and sentimental lips
into his beard.

O Cretan lying
in blue basalt: three
thousand layers: your kids
and nannies bleat in herds
of calcined curls and twists.

And I'll not dare
this strong-lipped sea: I
rockjump pool to pool, island
to coastline
where the rock sticks.

I vote for nothing
on the coast, but sea
and tea bag tea; where
little men with bellies dance
to metal melodies.

3

– On the green sheets your
sinewy arms,
reed flutes, played me down
where wind flew
at the sea like a cat

all afternoon behind
sea-hit shutters:
my name cried like a
forgotten spell: and he
likewise crying before.

In the sea's thirst
indifferent and lavish, on
the rocks, where the teenagers
dive and sun – the sea
like an old worker

swilling and spitting,
hawking the rock out,
cleaning its salt mouth out
roughly: the same yesterday
as tomorrow – there

(against that black ring
that scratched round full
towns last night its
government's reeking fire,
its closure –)

there, in your two
disunited ways
as if calling on caves
of witches, come bait
and drum me with

your wishes, both of you
crying out hoarsely
for the underwater clasp,
her frogskin tuned and turned
to golden sea.

Your sailors' voices
in low tones
along the coast
where water works its farm
and the oblivious children sun.

The separation

'Why can't you live together'
the boy asks.   He bends
away from the woman.
His profile is rigid, tired.
It's so late at night and
all evening they've quarrelled
and sworn, flung blue
murder of threats,
useless.   And
when she asks for
his real worries, not homework,
not school, not friends, he
in quiet asks.
She knows he knows her reply,
steely and more helpless than when
long ago he asked 'why
can't I?' and got
answered 'because you
can't.'   'Because we can't'
finally and finally she answers.

The prince of the shining white character armour

The prince of the shining
white character armour
came for me.

In the stretches of the night
he climbed, like a mole
winged bat, a master

of the staircase, hoof by
hoof – half winged,
his eyebrows
as clean as sycamore wings.

He covered my bed
because I couldn't sleep alone
I could not lie alone

and by him I toss and turn
uneasily.

His armour presses me, it
is so hard, so white,
it is alabaster and carapace.

By night I rub
the joints of the plates
removing shell dust with my hands

scraped and grazed . . .
Inclined over my mouth
that he calls out wonderful

that his fingers rub and whisk
that his mouth descends into
heavy, soft, dragging out my

tongue: inclined, he presses
my length to his breast and to
his flesh upraised

and lays
the armour
greave and plate and crest
on the floor beside the bed.

Stars go up and down

I rocket wildly and stars
are up and down
in my view
like eyes on stalks.
One day my mouth hangs
from yours, like a kitten,
pendulous, soft, your larger
pillow mouth my cave cat
my warm gospel.

Another day is another day.
We don't speak.   My eyes
hang on the floor
and you make yourself
a stiff sign of withdrawal
a huge dislike
I hate.

Like eyes bound, on stalks, we walk
past each other; whereas I know
            one finger touching,
yours on my hair or mouth or
            shoulder would
stroke the stars.

Leaves

Leaves at this time
turn to red and gold and pale
washed off and down

skins of leaves from trunks
shed, are flayed, float
leave the ploughing bark

his hands take hers
hold hers to the sky –
rain and light stick back the thin forms –

and raise up the hands
dropping and whirling, rising and prancing
white, exhausted; the wind
silently lays them back.

The cabin

No news in the honeycomb,
the old woman's cabin.
She is bound by choice in
white gauze, which he got from the chemist.

Now he's ill himself, his hair
an Eskimo out of the duvet
at nights, his body wet.
She can't sleep, takes white pills.

Some other times in the honeycomb
the sun in the crochet, the cabin
among thin buds on tree-tops,
she's light brown and giggles away under him.

The hypnotist's dream

The hypnotist made me dream:
I dreamt of glass darkness,
my oval abdomen
a sort of lady's mirror

a hand looking glass
swagged, with a china surround
but flat, on which swans
set out from peak

of bone to peak of bone.
Glass swans with raised heads,
red eyes and green wings
swam on the mirror of my belly.
    . . .
He frowns at this hypnotist's
dream: gets him nowhere
a hard hand mirror,
my skin a rink for swans?

All just a flat enclosed reflection.
Glass verbiage.
I am listing, scattering glints,
swans, sails after this blow.
    . . .
Further in
I recover.   The bone tiered
stadium.   Hill's edge, roof,
a limitless cavern.

An ice held mere in the dark
where he can fly in.
Where he follows,
 can melt, can melt in my arms.

The hawthorn

No   it's too much   this hand to
mouth
                but   listen my
darling, what choice have we?

Cooped up like two kids by
the witch
             ah   but no witch
nor giant spelled such gratings

Two thickened magpies branch
and flop
             through tanglewoods
we see in the pane

Go away to America   go I
shall live
             like a sow in
silk   when I live alone here

watching those thickhead magpies
wade
             through the black
stricken wooden hawthorn

Dear   what is your
countree

hold hands   when

Are there ever leaves?   Listen
outside
                the glass
                put your ear

not   not
overnight   ever?

Look up, look out

Anger
cool, calm and collected!
Not saying you bastard
but thinking it.

Look up, the New York statue
under her lightening points and
her outstruck arm holding the famed
fire: under her

heavy eyebrows she –
but only in the stone points of the
motionless eyes above the immigrants,
the pleaders of cases

or causes of liberty or right
coming in –
shows that kind of composed and
balancing dislike;

Which she personally is prepared
to put up with, and be
used for Athena or Justice
or Liberty or America or whatever.

Io the wanderer

I   sound of myself

O   O   the baby's two eyes over the cliff's edge
                              what have we here?
O..O..O   the helterskelter smotherfaced giggle in
answer to the big gruff What Have We Here?

O   say our mouths
                     our red tissues amazed
confident   crying our due   our
dutiful sound.
Words are hard
               clicking of rows of hard wooden words
in feeble will   in delicious silence
our red lips cried out, a child,
and look!   she's laced in magic beads
              she beams in amulets.

Vanity, smiles, fright in the
       moon's O
              tissues scared white
            (to a cow's white)

                    The increasing
salt cleft, the entranced and
    beguiled vault
              the moon's word
              (what have I here?)
Her bearing of the sun

Again and again daily and by century he
overbears her
that orange woodpecker terror
who pokes in and leans out on her
swaying elbow crook, her alder branch.
He skis wide out in deep space
        blue   green   black   burning   stippled
and striped cuckoo of the docile moon; and he
stings   jostles   taps the rump of the small
sparrow legged cow, till she flies
        puffa puff, round and round   round
galloping her stretches – she clops out
the thousands year rule of great man.

Far from being her baby
        he's rapidly a city, a field
        of teeth, from each one
jump   resplendent, fully armed missiles
and from each, a hundred warheads glitter.

So she flies through Europe, America, Asia and
at last in Egypt long before now, there so we
hear in peace from her tearing round, settled, lay
down on mud flats split by the sun's beak.

    Golden flies are beaming
    beneath a strobe light turning
    round and round, puffa puff.

There reads a small old sign:
    Crane Birds and Pygmies Fight Here
There reads a big glitterbugging sign:

FILL UP HERE LAST STOP TO VEGAS

Too late   too late

        The lunatic boy consults
        the glasseyed mollusc
        the lion lies down
        on his four gold paws

Hermit by the well's lip, by the lorries of diamonds
and topaz turning, she squeezes in, fits in, begins to speak:

of plump figs, strawberries and of
other hopeless fruit, of (with tears)
              her stunted girl
blind, rag round her flybit eyes
misted, the flies that home in her feet
and build a nest, lay their rich ripe white
stacks of prodigal and organised eggs
My daughter is a blind cripple
Demeter
        a girl aged
    O   her mouth says   O

      Io Io Io
the I and O formula
of the sun and the purple mollusc   of men
of armies   I   and my big mouth
those openwide red lips in delicious
silence   in fear

            What have I here
The lion lies down on her four paws
flickering by the wooden well's lip
the hermit carves her abacus   the boy's
lost perhaps forever   the old gold fly
           insists, we must be going on.

Dark

Everything's dark in the morning.
Just outside a phoenix
          begins to call
at quarter to six.

At blue before dawn
(coming over the bulk of the roofs)
it whistles like a child
lazily from the hawthorn.

It's bunked outside
          all night while
I have dreamt pain and all these
tears I can't get rid of.
Bird I can't see –
                   hear – can't see

Too far away

You are too far away
for my liking, my darling.

Three thousand miles of grey sea,
a watery chastity belt between us!

I want to cry but the tears don't
match that, the gulf

you opened, and locked
shut between us

the sea corset,
the huge shining belt.

The river, the child

And you   a chimera

a dozen horns   risky and impenetrable
in smoky bushes pearled with rain showers,
absurd too, in a boy's bunkbed
your feet stretching large cold and slender
over the edge

I fear and find
the chalk blue   dove grey
priest mask

my mouth I know is full of images
graven   chased (I am bold, see)
with bulls and monsters

but recently   I did dream
                of this birth:

              unlike your river
so green, swollen, punishing, roaring
swift, its icefloes carrying hippies
instruments flowers
and others carrying corpses, splayed
white on white
off white on white
livid on white   glass coffined
on the waters of turbulent downpouring.

Wax further smoothed by fur
                I had one child

he was born black and bullet headed:
his face and body slipped and slopped ivory
so easy   but then the head between
my legs   the waist garotted by bone
arse and spindle legs turn inside . .
A voice says lightly   *push   bear down*
his shoulders broad, damp and ivory
we obeyed and he slid from my cunt.
I shit him with strong ease   he stops between me.
Blank almond eyes eye back to me   the
black fringe over your brow.

Infant wreath   wreathèd   wraith child

    I woke up but the child
stays around   his eyes still into mine
he flexing ivory and bone and weight
(and softest   soft ear lobes   not to forget)

The loving red hen & the strong young fox

They're getting on fine
she's on her beam
he's crouching on the barn floor
she nods down, he springs up
For each a fine red feather
                a handsome red hair
each doodling in its comfortable place
       each in its air or earth
but each to the other   up   down
           swing high
                         swing low

Then despair crows up in him
He fixes on her more blatantly, aims
bang!   melts her, she wants whatever
                  a feather for a red red hair

So she loses her balance
Mama!   falls into the sack
It's a stone floor after all.

He never meant that
tells her off for letting him
stare her down like that
She knows it; only
sometimes her beak
gapes shrilly at his slant eyes
– she starts to sneer   oh your
floating autumn hide   oh your
     flashing titian hide   oh
yes maple leaved hair   oh

your ruff that embraces deep woods of snow
but I've no home to go now
but I can dance no more now
since you have broken my spring

He only meant, for his part
to eat in delicacy
to lick, to nibble
         Joy, hallowed
of the fox who munches up, the hen
    who's gone in . . .

and comes back later little by little, bit by bit?

She knows all that, she shared
the fever whining and snapping and shivering
between them in the air
                  between earth and beam

But now he has to starve.
Now there's only a stone in the sack
a broken hen statue
heroic embodiment of hen

a small chipped beauty   sad   sad

A feather floating out
                  for a red red hair

In the folk story, the Sly Young Fox traps the Little Red Hen into falling off her beam into his waiting sack . . . Later she escapes, replacing herself by a pile of stones . . .

Up to a sea blue door

Up to a sea blue door
his feet
running up the stairs
outside
clattering

Is this her visitor?
The old woman cries in bed
hearing
this approach

Now, outside the door
rearing
heavy as a horse
running amok in all its

unassuageable   good spirits

In corners, warmed
            circles of sun
                       tender to your hand
my pink skin

       You for a moment
           a corner
                lift
                      my bruised body

A window in the north, opened
      but the strong
                blustering gale

                will often quickly slam it shut

Leaves   podgy stars

Leaves   podgy   stars   hang
from my enemy the sycamore
It digs in under canals
and brick paths (It
    drains moisture from dry
bedded sinuses, from ironed out houserooms:
                         this headache
  conducting its splitting paths)
The leaves push   like small
                         horses
striving against water.

Where they are   on the
      branch it must
  be the oldfashioned
sea   the rough brown coarse
   sails of Dutch trawlers
      coming in steadily
                    raggledy
                    mast flags
bent and dashing on the east
wind   tenacious leaves

These boats
      don't chug out too far
the catch maybe down   but still
              hoards slither in
The trawlermen look ahead to a
horizon they make their own and
then they return.

Just occasional great black
                rebellious fishes
                wondrous fat, stubborn
                    inclinations
ambling   and stumbling

seas and seas and seas over

Gilbert's Motel

My long hair is flickering
in the rain storm
and the sky increases from black
to an entire devoted grey.

The brown pelicans
have inserted their
boat-like bodies, their broadswords
into the swamps

and equally the humans
here, into their boxes,
their bare lime bedrooms,
their big brown oldfashioned TVs.

I watch the creek, belted flat
mist out of green waves.
Over the bridge the trucks
hurdle and slap right on.

Key Largo, Florida, 1983

The pearly jawfish

raises its head
from a pebbly hole
like a minute square
peg, a prompter's
startled look, an
adjustable
            bollard.
With its pearly jaws
it shoves
coral rocks/ grit
from the hole's forecourt
(or in fright pulls one
down entire
on the jawfish itself).
Who sinks like
a finger puppet out of
sight.

           Up
wafts the peg head
staring, astral
up into air/ water,
a membranous phial
of translucent intestines:
the stop of the
bollard head imposes
on a smear
of lavender fin.
The silvery lower half
sends up
the jaws of pearl
to cry boo
but so nervy it drops

like a snubbed finger
a doomed soul, and
floats back to
its hole in the ground.

Key West town aquarium, 1983

Moon over Key West

1

West of Key West
hanging over the shot scarlet flares
the hibiscus tongues
of the sun gone down:
the emerald half moon.

Furry in the lights
on the pier, hides
of lions amble in, a
broken and ever flowing flesh
just out of conversation.

2

The frilled party streamers
of Christmas palm trees, smooth
cuffed, fanning no lady
but the sax blaring door
to Dirty Harry's, Captain Tony's.

I went to carouse under
Papa's large pale face
desperate in gravure.   Ernest
lost to fluorescent drums
which is Sloppy Joe's heart thumping.

I dived into that strip-lit
red and green kingdom, 'his
favorite bar'; but the jowls
quavered an undertone, sad,
deafened, a nostalgia

detailed, of the fish
bloodied pelt, the sea
he liked to mow down, out there
honey green, gulf blue
over the red green, strip-lit reef.

3
I saw four grey dolphins.
The first pushed a red football.
The second jumped a pole.
The third clapped his flippers,
the fourth, on antibiotics, wouldn't.

The sun rose, and the wind
all morning, through waisted
heavily dancing coconut palms.
I was loitering on the pier
by the pink and green Southernmost house.

South of Key West, the
white old man moon
hunches its back across shallows.
He wades between Man Key and
Mule Key, slowly far out.

Flipper at Key West

I saw four grey dolphins
the first poked a football
two clapped their flippers
three jumped a pole
the fourth, on antibiotics, wouldn't.

Really we had our mouths
open waiting for that
voluntary hurtling from here to
there, weight flicked up:
hooked on the red ball like them.

Forget the hop over the pole –
Solid ten foot muscled
dolphins entering a
slow triple leap, while
the fourth imitated weakly.

They don't escape, said our
loving yellow haired guide, they
like our dead fish too much.
Even a tinsy bit afraid of the
live snappers that teem here.

Now see Duffy 'targetting'
as we say, on Tracy's hand
– give Duffy a well earned round.
We do, heartily.   Remembering
'the upthrust of a dolphin

is like a nuclear missile'
admired the television man.
America salutes dolphins.
Out of the Base, US
defense against 'drugs and

communism' next door,
strides the new general:
the Navy calls on dolphins,
who still lead in sonics,
to train as underwater spies.

Outcry.   Duffy in the pen
clicks amiably on.
Tracy feeds fish in 'slidable'
chunks to the dolphins'
beige tongues.   And they

rove round the pool
after the show, surface,
heave back, twinkle an eye
sideways to inspect us
and glide down again, no interest.

Key West dawn

At once the dogs bark to each other;
but no wandering roosters, buried
by boulevards and carports.
The catbird mews in the pine feathers.

Last evening I drank myself
merrily with pink Seabreezes
into a night of the shivering horrors.
At the end: je ne regret rien.

Like an old lady's gold dress
the dawn embroiders the curtain.

Past an American classroom

Not water: it's a fluid   F-L-U-I-D
he bawled, sitting on the teacher's
desk, and the sperm, SWIM, yes
SWIM up the vagina.   I slinked
in my juicy flesh of mature
age past the open class door.
Flesh, FLESH, said my lover in
bed when I said, what's best, and
after that, your cunt, CUNT, and
after that, your ASS.   Hey what
about my face?   Comes a long way
after, but pretty, he murmurs.
The sperm teacher shot me a
swimmable glance, though his fierce
eyes saw just passing face flesh.
Somewhere I'm joined, I guess.
The girl and boy students take steadily
their notes of their joinable
bodies.

Key West

Watching American TV

I kept turning back to the preacher.
She was still at the mike
an hour later.   I liked her
tiptilted nose, her ambiguous glossy
black hair, I liked the
dove to eagle of her husky
voice, the breathy
listing of endless severe complaints
when she was sixteen, which afforded
her severe pains in the foot, ribs and
chest area, till faith healing to
her amazement   'Ah never would've
b'lieved'   made it all possible, to
stand before the mike in crippling
heels for an hour shouting
hosannas from great lungs
at a TV crowd of
millions, including yours truly
amazed.

Said the judge

Said the salvage court judge
in the 1850s, there's
something fishy about
half the wreckers I deal with . . .
Key Westers fought ants and
hurricanes so as to swing
pink glass chandeliers
above their curved dining tables.
Cargoes coaxed thus, fixed
by oblivious dim lightings
on the outer reefs, slip
in to sweeten the homes
of the wealthiest, the most correct.
Ah, says young Alberta, handling a
silk length, palest water marked,
a northerly rosebud tint straight
from Paris, hardly water or salt
stained: What new joys
Papa, from the reef today?
Surprise me! Do!   She puts
up Brussels made lace mittens before
her blue eyes.
Play your scales, Miss, on
our new rosewood pianoforte from Hamburg
and mind your prying.   That
took forty lives.   I want to
see your little fingers glide over
its white keys like
our gentle angelfish in and out
of coral.

Key West

Vieux Carré

The first room was sunny with
flounces, overlooked a stranger's pool blue
green with banana plants.   Steps
climbed to a dozen galleries.
I couldn't hop, skip our green

stairs.   You called me Blanche Dubois
in the second room, inside
coral flounces and claret red plank
walls where we guessed slaves
had once lived.   I wept,

argued, admitted your pointed
hard-loving tongue.   In a salon
a butch boy entwined with
his small python, showed it off,
its head roved and flickered, a baby doll.

I walked out by the corner
bar, even at dawn smoky and
pounding inside; the odd van
or man down Dumaine, leaning by:
'Come with me?   Anything you like

laid on.'   I shrug him off, yawn
– what a night, hour after
hour of men zagged heel to
head like a black brown white
python twined on my flounces –

I delicately lick my dried lips

Young men up in the birdcage
galleries, always with thin hips
and sandy moustaches, embrace
passionately.   Light cooling it,
amber as skin through upstairs leaves.

New Orleans, 1983

Let's pretend

      When things
have shot past the mile end:
the runway into the sea or
the mountain: no lift-off.
Then we'll pretend the
clouds thinned
through the wings, that
the city of the goldstick
lanterns, voltage blurred
like crocus flowers in thousands
ordered over the damp hills
      and the bay,
fell back into dusk (with
such a surprising glow)
and that two such dear
lovers can fly back
where we came from, backwards
into the sunset.

San Francisco, April 1983

What idiots lovers are

You meet a man
as tall as a redwood
as sly as a garrulous blue jay
as patient as a riding-horse.
You're scalding, your love's boiling
over – it surely is but
only sometimes.   He's the same,
boiling –
same cauldron of
frangipani blossoms and toads
– The distance between the
two idiots narrows
to Achilles' tortoise.   What
a puffing.   And
then it stops – they
look down between their
toes, mingled – and each stands
wobbling on opposite sides.
What immense landscapes, canyons,
chasms, torrents pour between
these ten and ten toes.
Too great – the vertigo
is insufferable, the lovers cling, lean
clasp like a church steeple, harder
and harder the cement, the
tongue and groove, the pebble and dash
– the vane cock dances in every
possible quarter, reconciliations,
rebirths.   The pit underneath splits
the great tower
in the end, how can it not?
                      Helter skelter
you see the redwood heave and totter

the smashed jay feathers, the
horse hoof over ear,
the lot curl so slowly down
as if air could hold fancies
and their lovers up forever,
ball-eyed, clamped, grooved.
Pit-props – that's what
they make.   Idiots of lovers
trying out edifices.

San Francisco 1983

I said goodbye to you

I said goodbye to you
on the sadder side of the Atlantic
that for taking off and flying away

but really I left you in San Francisco
between one bounce and the next hill

or I left you in New Orleans
in the Vieux Carré
piano-playing under some flowered gallery

or even right down in Key West
with your father's Columbian hat
on your head, and a pipe, pointing
out to Cuba and remembering the whores
of Batista's time genially
though you'd gun run
for Castro given half a chance

and a hundred thousand bucks
– you'd say.
              That's the sort of thing
you said.   I used
   to like it and laugh.   How
you touched a nerve in locked
   up shy places and
had me laugh, at your fingertips.

Cry.   There's no touchdown
for thousands of sea miles
or so; then just well gone over
raked, over pastured dust
to scrabble in again and
try to sow.

Cry.   My seed in you got nowhere,
yours savaged me out of
its under rage, and died
and left me like this
absorbed in my barrenness.

No touchdown.   This
plane flies and flies into cold.

The woman alone

1

Deserted and not visited
by women, her own mother old,
here is a sad picture.
Why am I excluded?   (She asks.)
Why the bread knife
        prickling against my finger?
The sharp meat knife
all through
has earned me such
exclusion.   They're
not there, the busy bees,
the chatterers.
Men!   That's it,
(she thinks over and over) they're
jealous, but why?   They
have their well fleshed homes
their cows and acres . . .

The Nurse-shark-toothed
        following sirens
(she sang to weakly, hour in, hour out)
          insanely:
they'll not let me get away,
they're closed ranks, and the famous
golden hair has branched
to a lacquered fence, the mirrors
coagulate when I look:
they round to bullets.

(She has the idea of being followed
inserted, like a tooth or a comb
        into the wrong head.)

Was it a lie (she wonders)
or a magic wish, the
woman who loved a woman?
No, she has met them.

2

Is it me?   (She asks,
asking herself as if to a judge
– but who else is there?)
She's aware of her own
lacquered stockade – her
own palace of doped sleep.
                The push up
her garden path is in
all justice, not (she still
thinks) not so thorny,
not so hard-won.   Then,
                the palace:

(here her heart turns to lead)
the place itself is wrong,
sparse, an illusion, no
carpets and nothing in the
kitchen?   (Her heart keeps melting,
the lead tears squeeze out.)

                The dwelling
(she must not cry like this:
her mother is too old)
is good.   It will
be visited in due course.
(She was going to run away.)
The house is sound, reasonably
                stocked
no incandescent waking palace
but sound.   (She
wanted to run away.)

3

She lights a fire
on stones blackened
by years of use:
to know where
to come back to.

She walks into the wood
with red hood
and basket, and bow
and silver thonged
ankles: O huntress of women!
(My mother lies in there, living still.)

As we might have done

Your hand . . .
              octopus slipping
my breasts, my waist arched
raised, hollowed, open
pulled to you

            if you could have lain here

This childish and longing starfish
expansive to north and south
east and finally west

            your weight
warm as the sea, as a
sea beast rubbing and moving, as
a horse moving in the shade
in the corner of a field, leg
to leg

            as we might have done